DON'T SCHEDULE YOUR WEDDING

on Game Day

Charlotte Barnes

PublishAmerica
Baltimore

ISBN: 1-4137-9235-9
PUBLISHED BY PUBLISHAMERICA, LLLP
www.publishamerica.com
Baltimore

Printed in the United States of America

My whole family watches football. My father watches football. My brother watches football. My mother watches football. I came by my obsession naturally. I think if I hadn't liked football, they would have taken me back to the hospital, even if I had been twelve years old, and said, "Doctor, this isn't our child. This can't be our child. She doesn't like football."

Even if they didn't take me back to the hospital, they might have made me the black sheep of the family and when visitors came over, they would have said, "Oh, we don't talk about her much. She stays at the back of the house. She doesn't like football."

Luckily, no hospital returns, exiles, or exorcisms were needed. I did love football. In fact, I can't really remember a time when I didn't love football. I pulled for the Dallas Cowboys when I was young. I added the University of Alabama to my list of beloved teams, and found comfort in that distinctive hat, spotted on a Saturday afternoon sideline.

I really found the love of my life, though, in April 1984. Yes, the word "axiom" has special meaning to me, because it's the word that made me my county's representative in the Big Bend Regional Spelling Bee, and put me on the road to my first trip to Tallahassee. I still remember my first glimpse of Florida State University's Doak Campbell Stadium. The garnet edifice rose in metallic majesty in the Tallahassee dusk, the proud logo on the press box. I was enthralled, just absolutely enchanted, and knew then, in that moment, that place was where I belonged.

I didn't win the spelling bee, but I took something far more precious than a trophy or a ribbon with me when I left Tallahassee the next day. I had motivation. I had dreams. My goal from that time on was to do well enough that I could get a scholarship so that I could attend Florida State University.

To be honest with you, I had very little adjustment to make as far as motivating myself to try to achieve my goal. You see, I was born two months premature, and due to some physical limitations, it was always clear to me that I was going to have to focus that much more, work that much harder, when others might be tempted to coast along.

When I finally made it to Florida State University in the fall of 1989, I was euphoric. It was an adjustment, there was a little homesickness, but I made wonderful friends at Florida State. It soon became clear to many of my friends in Landis Hall what a football fanatic I was. Some even joked that I was probably going to wind up getting married during the half at one of the ballgames!

I still remember how much I enjoyed walking from my dorm to Doak Campbell Stadium. All the tailgaters would be out, dressed in their garnet and gold. We do love our paraphernalia at Florida State.

I always sat on the alumni side because I was serious about watching the game. I wasn't concerned with who was flirting with whom in the student section, or how long it was going to take the guy with the little plastic bags of beer to get caught. I would stand by the fence at Gate 2, and wait for the stadium to open, which was generally about two hours before kickoff. Some may think me crazy for wanting to sit in an empty stadium for two hours before the game, but I found that it became one of my favorite rituals. There's an almost spiritual quality to the whole experience, as you sit in the stadium, with the sun kissing your face and the wind gently blowing in your hair. In those moments before the game, I felt at peace and full of excitement at the same time. Even as I'm sitting here writing this, I'm getting excited just reliving that experience. I'm just giddy over Florida State football. I've never found anything quite like it.

I follow other teams, of course, and love to watch the teams of the Southeastern Conference, and I know that there are many fans out there who understand what I'm saying.

That is why I've written this book. Fans of the game understand that there is more to the game we love than just men in pads and helmets knocking the crap out of each other. Football can teach us, or at least reinforce the lessons Mama and Daddy taught us, about the importance of teamwork, humility, persistence, and discipline. That's just for starters. I'm not claiming to have covered every life lesson football can teach us, but I've collected some of the lessons that were important to me.

To all the coaches, players, fans, and friends who find joy between the white lines, bless you. With love I present to you, *Don't Schedule Your Wedding on Game Day.*

DON'T SCHEDULE YOUR WEDDING
on Game Day

Let me be honest. I find myself actually resenting friends and relatives who schedule their weddings on game day. Heck, I would miss my own wedding if Florida State and Miami were playing each other. Hey, whom am I kidding? I would never schedule my wedding from August to January, anyway. With six other months to pick from, why be so cruel?

I do realize that there are some people out there who don't give a fig if their wedding falls on a game day. I'm betting they're not from Alabama, though. However, if they do go ahead and schedule their weddings on game day, they are increasing the likelihood that people like me will skip the wedding, or show up with headphones resenting the heck out of them.

LAYER
Your Clothes

Mama always told you to layer your clothes, right? If she didn't, you would figure it out as you sat in the sun with the teeming masses of cheering humanity. You'll want to be able to take off that jacket if you need to. You can take more off if you have on too many layers. Once you're at the game, you're stuck with whatever weather Mother Nature throws at you. Be as comfortable as you can.

TEAMWORK
Is Important

One person cannot win a game. Without all eleven players working together, you go from "red zone" to "dead zone." The same holds true in everyday life. Whether it's members of a unit at your job, or members of a family at home, you make the most progress in life by working together.

DISCIPLINE
Is Important

Discipline is often what separates Mr. Superior from Mr. Mediocre. Mr. Superior realizes that in order to be successful on game day, he must come to practice, eat the right foods, get enough sleep, and study the plays, blocking schemes, or film to obtain adequate knowledge to succeed. You can't achieve if you don't believe. Mr. Superior knows that the discipline he exhibits, the sacrifices he makes, will lead to success. The same holds true in life. Sometimes you must give up what you'd like to do, to do what you know you must do.

Also, a player's lack of discipline may hurt his teammates on game day. Think of a lineman who keeps lining up in the neutral zone. He is getting his team penalized. He's hurting not just himself, but others, too.

RULES
Are Important

Rules are important because they keep us from degenerating into chaos. Think how wild a game would be if there were no rules. Rules keep us straight on the football field, and in life. We may not agree with all of them, but like quarterbacks or coaches arguing with an official, we say our piece and let it go, or we take it up later with those who have the power to get the rule changed.

PEOPLE WANT TO BE WITH PEOPLE
Who Are like Themselves

Football fans like to spend time with other football fans. They have football parties, go to sports bars, tailgate, or head to the games in droves, just to be together.

People like to be with people with whom they can have "I do, too!" moments.

"I like Mexican food!"

"I do, too!"

"I always wanted to travel to Greece."

"I do, too!"

Football games are thousands of people in stadiums, and millions of people at home, have a "I do, too!" moment.

WEAR
Sunscreen

It is very important to wear sunscreen when you go outside. It's not very enjoyable to bring your sunburn home from the game. So screen before you scream.

Managing Time
Is Very Important

I have wanted to strangle many a player or coach when time is running off the clock, the team needs a score, and they saunter up to the line like they're just sliding up to a fast food counter to order a combination meal. Wasting time can cost you a game. Wasting time is a crime in football.

Of course, some people function on what I call Never Gonna Do Better Time, because they are never going to do better than they're doing now, because of a lack of a sense of urgency in their actions. Successful people have a sense of urgency. Do it now, do it now, do it now.

SHOW RESPECT
for Others

I don't believe in trash talking about other teams or their fans. They may not support the same team you do, they may even be obnoxious, but show them respect. They have just as much right to believe in their team, as you do to believe in yours. Let your team kick their team's butt on the field, and that will be enough.

You will not always agree with everyone in life, but have enough maturity, and enough respect for each other, to agree to disagree.

ALWAYS Do Your Best

Whenever a player goes out on the field, he goes out intending to do his best.

Whatever activity you participate in, always do your best. You don't want to look back at your life later and have regrets, wishing you had tried harder when you had a chance to do something.

A LARGE PART OF SUCCESS
Is Mental

I believe that football games are won in two places. They are won on the line of scrimmage during the game. They are won in the minds of the players before and during the game.

I am convinced that there have been many games where two teams have equal talent, but one team triumphed because it was mentally stronger than the other. Earlier I said you couldn't achieve if you don't believe. Players must believe they can win that game on that day. They must not let anything such as trash talking get into their heads. Trash talking is just a silly way for people to get you out of your game. This is where maturity can come in handy. Mature, intelligent people see trash talk for what it is and can ignore it. It means nothing.

People talk a lot of junk in football and in life. Believe in yourself, in your values and goals, and kick butt.

NEVER Give Up

If a football team gave up every time they got behind, there'd be no point in watching the rest of the game. One of the greatest comebacks I ever witnessed was Florida State's game versus the University of Florida in 1994. They were beating us 31 to 3. When I got home to watch a taped replay, the announcers were thanking the sponsors in the third quarter! My beloved team did not lose hope, and they came back to tie the score at 31. That tie felt like a win to us fans! Even when things look rough in life, never give up.

Awards Are Nice, but They Don't Always Translate to Future Success

It's nice to get an award, but it doesn't always translate to a successful professional sports career. The same thing is true in life. Enjoy the award in the spirit it's given, and continue to work hard, because an award's not a guarantee of future success.

You Can Be Successful and Nice *at the Same Time*

There are plenty of football players and coaches who are successful in a very competitive field, yet they maintain their core value system. You can be successful and nice at the same time. I wish more people in the working world understood this. We have all met people who get big heads because they are the regional managers of whatever. Why should I respect that, particularly if I know for a fact they got there by stabbing others in the back? Remember in God's eyes we are all the same.

DON'T REST
on Past Achievements

Last year was last year. This year's a whole new ballgame. We've all seen teams who seem to lack enthusiasm. They seem to assume that because they were good last year, they're going to be good this year. This leads to the effort not being put in to continually improve.

What can we learn from this? Don't become complacent. Don't rest on past achievements. Always strive to become the best version of yourself that you can be. To be anything else would be a tragedy for you, and a loss for the world.

YOUR CIRCUMSTANCES
Affect Your Actions

Actions that are acceptable at football games, such as screaming, or dressing in costumes, may not be acceptable at your workplace. Of course, I guess it would depend on your workplace. If your workplace encourages screaming and dressing in costumes, I want to see it. On second thought, maybe I don't.

TAKING TURNS
Is Important

In football if my offense can't do anything in three downs, they generally use the fourth down to punt the ball to the other team to see if they can do anything with it. Both teams get their chances to see what they can do. From the time we are old enough to understand our language, we are taught to share and to take turns. Who hasn't been told during his childhood, "Let Lucy have a turn on the swing," or "Let Johnny play the video game for a while"?

HAVING A PLAN
Is Important

If a football team went onto the field with no plan whatsoever, they would probably also have to have little expectation of success, right? We would not want to eavesdrop on our team's offense in the huddle and hear our quarterback say, "I'm just going to throw the ball in the air and hope to God someone catches it."

If we don't want our football team going into a stadium without a plan, we certainly don't want to go into our daily lives without a plan.

What are we hoping to accomplish in our day? How might we accomplish these goals? One of my favorite things to do is to write down a list of tasks that I need to accomplish. I'll even put a few really easy ones on the list. After each task is completed, I'll scratch it off, and it gives me a real feeling of accomplishment, as I can actually see the tasks I've completed. One time I checked my purse and I had three little memo pads in it! While I'd really like to say that I had expectations of filling all those memo pads with accomplished tasks, I honestly just needed to clean out my purse. One memo pad at a time is all that's needed.

ADJUST
Your Plan

The best coaches look at what's going on during the game and adjust what they are doing to better utilize their teams' assets to lead them to victory. If the long bomb's not working, try something else. If they're leaving a receiver wide open in the center of the field, take advantage. Do not be afraid to change your plan as new opportunities present themselves. If your dream job was offered to you, would you say, "Sorry that wasn't in my plan"? That's too rigid a way of thinking. If big changes scare you, start slowly. You're not going to see a rainbow if you won't look outside your window.

Doing the Same Thing All the Time Can Be Boring

If a football team is always running the same plays, it becomes boring for the fans to watch. Also, the opposing teams' defenses will be able to stop the offense from scoring because they already know what play they are going to run.

If you are always doing the same things the same way all the time, it might be time to shake things up a bit. Try a new restaurant, take a different route home, or cook a new enticing dish that you've been meaning to try. A rut can seem comfortable, but you have to climb out every now and then.

A Good Defense
Is Important

A good defense is a thing of beauty. A good defense is important because it helps keep the opposing team's offense from scoring, so that keeps the pressure off its own offense. Ball control is what it's all about. If the defense keeps the other team's offense off the field, then that gives its own offense more time with the ball. If the other team doesn't have the ball, that lessens the chances of a score, and if they can't score, we can win.

As you've gone through your own life, you may have encountered many areas of life in which a good defensive strategy came in handy. It may have been in tense business meetings, on the road as a defensive driver, or even when overcoming a potential or real physical threat.

SEIZE
the Day

In football, you have to be alert for opportunities. A player might fumble, a kick could be blocked, or a quarterback could make a bad pass. Those who succeed in football are always open to the opportunities of life, just like a running back slipping through a hole knocked by his offensive linemen.

In life, an opportunity could come your way at any time. Be ever watchful, and take that chance when it comes your way.

SHOW CLASS
in Victory

There are few things I dislike more than showboating. Even though I'm a young person, I'm kind of "old school" in my values, and I believe that when you make a good play, or even a touchdown, you should act like you've done it before. I'm not saying you shouldn't be happy or excited, but I don't go for all this dancing in the end zone and stuff like that. Some of the antics are downright silly, and even classless. I also don't like braggarts, or people who talk about being there to "showcase their talents."

I believe the media sometimes gets these kids to say things in the heat of the moment, and then uses the quotes in an inflammatory fashion. I believe that if players must talk to the media, then the only thing they should say is, "We're going to do our best and hope for a good game." Even if a team's talent is infinitely superior to the talent on the opposing team, a player should never say, "I'm going to pound them into the ground and make them sorry they even came out on the same field with me!"

The same lesson can be taken into our lives as fans and people. Be humble, modest, and thankful. Win with class, don't be an ass.

SHOW CLASS
in Defeat

The media loves to show people when they're upset. "If you're in despair, the media's there," should be their motto. If a person's not upset when they get there, they'll ask questions to make him upset. In football, it's hard to take a loss. Everyone works so hard during the week, and then, for one reason or another, the team loses. Instead of being able to grieve the loss privately, the players often have to deal with stupid questions from the media, such as, "How do you feel about the loss?"

I think players should have a stock answer to questions from the media. If their before the game spiel was, "We're going to do our best and hope for a good game," their answer for a loss should be, "We did the best we could. Of course, we're disappointed in a loss, but we're going to take this as a learning experience and an opportunity to improve. We give all the credit in the world to the other team's players and coaches. They just outplayed us tonight."

What kind of loser are you? Turn a loss into a win by putting the lessons of the day within. Ask yourself, "How can I improve? What can I learn from the fact that Jimmy beat me out for the promotion to Paper Shuffler II?"

Be Patient
and Good Things Will Happen

As a young kid coming onto a football team, you sometimes have to practice hard and wait until it's your turn to start. There are older, more experienced guys ahead of you. If you continue to do your best to improve, you'll get your shot.

The same holds true in life. Sometimes you have to wait for an opening for that transfer to another unit or that shot at a promotion. If you don't have that patience and that desire to persevere, then maybe a new team or job is for you.

IT'S FUN
to Dress Up

It's fun to dress up to go to a ballgame. You can paint your face or put on a temporary tattoo. You even see people with extremely elaborate costumes. Of course, near Christmas, you always have a few people dressed as Santa Claus at the games.

Some of us also like to dress up at work when Halloween comes around. Now, I wasn't that into Halloween years ago, but in the last several years, I've really begun to like dressing up.

HARD WORK
Pays Off

Before you get in the game, you've got to put in the pain. You have to work hard at practice, take time to study plays and film, and do a hundred of other little things that it takes to be good. That requires sacrifices. You're going to have to get up earlier in the morning than you would have liked to get to the classes you need to work around practice. You may have to miss some parties or some outings with your friends in order to study or write a paper because you didn't get a chance due to practice.

You have to make some of the same sacrifices in a job environment. If you want a bonus or a promotion, you must work hard. Think of the story you read as a child about the differing work philosophies of the grasshopper and the ant. In order to succeed, you must be an ant.

PRIORITIES
Are Important

This goes along with the previous message about hard work. You must have priorities both in life and football. In football, on the field you have to know what's important to you in the game. According to which team your team is playing, some of the priorities may change, but the main two are to score and to stop the other team from scoring.

Even as fans every college football Saturday, we have to see who's playing and decide which games we want to watch the most. Personally, I have to catch Florida State and Alabama.

Setting priorities at work will also serve you well. When you are overloaded with tasks, you have to decide which tasks most need accomplishing on this particular day. A list is helpful, and gives you a sense of accomplishment as you check things off.

At work, home, or on the football field, priorities help keep us on the path to success. People will feel less stressed if they know what their main goals are and how they are going about achieving them.

EVERYONE
Makes Mistakes

People have a disturbing tendency to forget their own mistakes when jumping on others for theirs. On the football field, a ball may be fumbled, an interception thrown, coverage blown, or a kick missed. Before you go jumping on others, ask yourself, "Haven't I ever made a mistake?" Sure, mistakes can be frustrating, but sometimes a kid's state of mind gets even worse because now he's dwelling too much on the kick he just missed, instead of concentrating on the ones he's got to make now. Since I'm mentioning kicking, I'd like to say that in the end, it should not have to come down to the kicker saving the game. It is the offense's responsibility to get the football in the end zone. It's no wonder these kids miss occasionally, with the tremendous pressure that's put on them.

You have made mistakes in your life. We all have. Remember that as you deal with others each day.

COUNTING
Is Important

From the time you were a little tyke, people were teaching you how to count. In football counting is important because you have to make sure you have the correct number of players on the field, or your team can get penalized.

In life, you need to count money. If you're like me, you also count the minutes until five o'clock on a workday.

NEVER DRINK A BIG DRINK
Before a Big Game

You know that if you drink that big drink before the game, you are going to have to go to the bathroom. It's usually at the most pivotal part of the game.

People drink big drinks at the movies, and always have to get up during the good parts. They drink stuff on car trips, knowing that they're going to have to stop, and probably in the middle of nowhere.

In summary, control your consumption to stop your peeing compunction. If you don't, you're going to chance missing that big play.

SUCCESS
Spoils People

Success spoils people. Players start becoming complacent, if they don't watch out. Fans start becoming demanding, and if the team doesn't have a ten-win season, they act like it's a flop. They now expect ten wins, darn it!

Fight against becoming complacent in your life. Always work hard and enjoy the success while it lasts. Be thankful that you're in a position to be successful.

You Can Succeed, Regardless of Your Station in Life

Football is full of stories of players who came from difficult circumstances, but became successful. What can we take from this?

It doesn't matter what your station in life is. If you find your talent and work hard, you can be successful. There are even different definitions of success. I believe that if you treat others with respect and kindness, you are a success, regardless of your station in life.

Be the Best You Can Be, Wherever You Are

Whether you're the water boy, the trainer, or the quarterback, be the best you can be wherever you are. Your success helps make team success.

Some players may not be starters yet, but they contribute in practice or as substitutes, and their commitment helps make them, and the others around them, better.

If you aren't doing your best in life, you're holding up your own development. At work, you would not say, "I'm only a Paper Shuffler I, so I'm not going to try."

Always strive to be the best version of yourself.

NOT EVERYONE
Can Be First String

Every player can't come to a team and start. There are only eleven players from your team out there at one time. The whole team may actually be around eighty or so players. That means some people are not starting. Get used to that in football and in life. Continue to work hard, and regardless of what happens, strive to be the best you can be.

THERE ARE THINGS
More Important Than Money

Despite the fact that it seems to hold a lot of importance today, there are things more important than money. You can even see it in football. There's tradition, loyalty, and friendship. Plus, when players get hurt, you realize their health is more important than money.

Sometimes in life, we have to make decisions about what's more important to us. Is it money or our health? Is it money or our family? Is it money or our mental and emotional health? It goes back to setting priorities in life. Ask yourself, "What's more important to me than money?"

FIND
Your Talent

In football, teams are full of players who play certain positions because they, or their coaches, realized at some point that the player could excel in the skills needed to play that position. If they tried to play another completely different position, they may not do quite as well.

Just as young players find their talents, their places, on a football team, people find their talents and their places, in life.

Where do you excel? You may have multiple unexplored talents. Leave no talent untapped. You're always striving to be the best version of yourself, with all your many gifts.

ANTICIPATE

the Actions of Others.

In football, in order to make a good plan for a game, it's good to have an idea what the other team is going to be doing. Based on the study of previous game film and action during the game, a skillful strategist anticipates the actions of others. It's similar to the work of a good general in battle. A large part of the appeal of football is the enjoyment of the strategy and execution of the plays. It's not just a bunch of guys in helmets and pads knocking the crap out of each other.

This same idea of anticipation of the actions of others can be applied to your own life. Humans are creatures of habit. If you watch and listen to them long enough, you will be able to figure out what they are going to do in most situations. This is good defensive, as well, as offensive strategy, for life, as well as football.

STUDYING
Is Important

Studying game film is an important part of planning a football team's strategy. Therefore, studying is important for football.

Students have to study to do in well in class. Studying is important for students.

It is important in every aspect of life. If you are willing to put in the time and effort, you can learn almost anything you want to know.

THERE'S A DIFFERENCE
Between School Spirit and Vandalism

I love my alma mater, but there is a difference between school spirit and celebrating a victory and vandalism. I would never go down on the field and help tear down a goal post. Tearing down a goal post is vandalism. That goal post is not the property of those individuals, and therefore, they are guilty of committing a crime. The media shows it happening and rarely does an announcer have the gumption to call it what it is. If I painted my team's name on someone else's car, they wouldn't call it school spirit. It's vandalism.

The World Does Not Stop
Because of a Ballgame.

I hate to say this, but the world does not revolve around football. It's true, but it was very painful for me to admit, so let's just move on.

BUILD

a Strong Foundation

At the beginning of this book, I talked about the importance of layering your clothes. It is just as important to build a strong foundation. I'm talking about wearing comfortable undergarments here. You're going to spend hours sitting down, standing up and cheering and goodness knows what else, so it is very important to be comfortable.

For me, this one means no uncomfortable stuff, such as thongs. I just can't even like the idea of them. If I were wearing a thong, I'd feel like Florida was covered, but the rest of the nation was left open for attack. I like a little more coverage on my back forty.

PHYSICS
Is Important

Force, velocity, and momentum are all important in football. Ask a guy who just got the crap knocked out of him by a linebacker if it wasn't important. Ask a kicker whose kick falls short if force wasn't important.

The laws of physics are at work all through our lives. Our bodies are in motion, our cars move on freeways, and we throw a ball with the neighbor's boy.

GEOMETRY
Is Important

Ask any kicker who's kicked a wide right if angles aren't important.

Geometry is all around you. It was used to build the house you're living in right now. If angles weren't measured properly, your house wouldn't fit together properly, and would probably be falling around your head right now.

Keeping Up with Documents
Is Important

Your football ticket is like a magic key to Joy Land. Keeping up with it keeps you in the game.

From the time your teacher pinned a note to Mom on your sweater, or they pinned a construction paper bluebird on your shirt to remind tiny you to ride the "bluebird bus," you have had to keep up with documents. You know it's important. You also know there are a lot of people out there who are lucky their heads haven't caught on fire from the rocks in their brains rubbing together.

Keep up with your tickets, folks. I'm not giving you mine.

Bring EVERYTHING that You're Going to NEED with You

A common stadium policy is "no readmittance." If you leave the stadium, you can't come back in. Bring all you need with you or do without.

SHARE
What You Have

Tailgaters are nice folks. People have a chance to share some food, do the whole, "Where y'all from?" thing, and enjoy a little togetherness with those of like mind. They may not know you when you get there, but they'll know you before you go.

PEOPLE LOVE
to Get on Television

Football fans will yell, hold up their baby, stick up their homemade signs, paint their bald heads, dress up or down, or pretty much do anything else they can so Mom and Dad can see them on television. Players do it, too. They dance, do silly moves, yell "Hi, Mom!" or anything else they can to get attention.

SOME PEOPLE SHOULDN'T BE IN JOBS
Where They Have to Deal with Other People.

Some coaches shouldn't be in coaching. They have bad, violent temper tantrums, can't deal with the media, can't talk to the kids, and can't deal with their coworkers. Some people should not be in positions where they are supervising other coaches or players. They don't have the personalities for it. They liked football, and thought they should coach. They should really be hermits. There's nothing wrong with not wanting to deal with people, but you have to be aware enough to know and deal with your own tendencies.

DELEGATION OF DUTIES
Is Good

I'm not good at delegating. I either hate asking the person to do something or don't trust that they'll do it.

Football coaches must delegate. They hire assistants to handle certain aspects of coaching the kids and expect those assistants to perform those duties faithfully. Also, head coaches have many demands on their time, They give speeches, talk to the media, deal with the Athletic Director, sign pictures, and so on. That's all in addition to their coaching responsibilities. The ultimate responsibility lies with the head coach.

You Don't Judge a Book by Its Cover,

so Don't Judge a Fan by His Covering

Just because someone is wearing the shirt of a team that you do not like, don't assume the person is a jerk or someone you can't like. There are many examples of "mixed marriages," of people who pull for opposing teams. Be mature enough to agree to disagree.

PICK UP
After Yourself

Do not leave your trash at the stadium or in the parking lot. Pick up after yourself. You wouldn't want someone coming to your house and throwing down his trash, would you?

BE CONSIDERATE
of the Person Next to You

The person in the seat next to you has come to watch and enjoy a football game. They have not come to prop up your drunk behind, get doused with your soda, or to get hit in the head with your homemade sign. Please think of those around you.

WATCH
Your Language

I know that emotions can run high during a ballgame, but would you want a child to hear and repeat what you're saying? Be considerate of the sensibilities of those around you. You're intelligent enough to express yourself without cursing, aren't you?

If People Are Irritating at Home, They're Going to Be Irritating at the Stadium

Some people just can't leave you alone to watch a game in peace. If they can't stop asking questions and messing with you at home, then don't expect a miraculous personality transformation when you take them to the stadium. That'll hold true wherever you take them.

SOME PEOPLE
Have
Hidden Artistic Talents

Football games bring out people's hidden artistic talents. Some people, who don't even draw in their regular daily lives, show up at a ballgame with elaborate, unique homemade signs. They even paint their bald heads. It does make you wonder about the guy sitting next to you at work. What could he do if he tried?

PEOPLE WILL PUT UP WITH SOME BAD WEATHER

to Do Something They Love

Watch some games on television. People will sit out in a pouring rain, fog, or blizzard to watch football. Hats off to people in places like Green Bay or Buffalo. I'd be sitting at home hoping the game wasn't blacked out.

MAMAS AND DADDIES
Love to Brag

During slow game action, the media will drag out Mama and Daddy to talk about their son who's playing in the game. They'll be wearing the son's jersey number, or buttons with his picture on them.

But you already knew Mama and Daddy like to brag, didn't you? You hear parents every day at work or in the grocery store line.

Kids Like to Say "Hi" to Moms

Watch any camera put on almost any team bench in America, and at least one kid is going to say "Hi" to Mom. It's actually a refreshing change from the usual "We're Number One!" or "They Can't Stop Me!" I do wish kids would thank Dad now and then, though.

"ADULT" Does NOT Necessarily Mean MATURE

Just because these kids are technically adults, doesn't mean they're mature. All the talking trash, dancing in the end zone, and all that other stuff is silly. The fans do silly stuff, as well. Go to any gathering in America and observe people and you'll see this one holds true.

ONE PERSON
Can Make a Difference

In football, one person can make a difference. All it takes is one person stepping up and doing something great to change the momentum of a game. Think of all the great interceptions made during a game.

One person can make a difference in the lives of others. You may not even realize it, but something you say during a conversation with another person could have a profound effect on them. Try to always be positive and encourage others. Be a force for good.

WALKING
Is Good for You

One of my favorite rituals on game day would be my walk from my campus dorm to the stadium. I have always found that walking, along with other activities involving movement, helps stimulate my thinking. I got a lot of good thinking done between Landis Hall and Doak Campbell. I miss those walks.

Some Things Can't Be Explained

Why do people feel attracted to one team over another? Why was I so profoundly changed by my trip to Tallahassee as a youngster? Some things can't be explained; they're just feelings.

PEOPLE
Are Fickle

Some people are fickle. They claim to be for one team, but they change according to how the team's doing or the direction of the wind that day. These people are a dangerous lot in the workplace, as well. They'll change allegiances according to who is in power, regardless of whether the new leader has any integrity or character.

QUIET TIME

Is Nice

I am an introvert. I find that my personal batteries recharge more quickly with a little quiet time. I have to retreat when I find all the stimulation the extroverts enjoy too taxing. I found an almost spiritual quiet in the empty stadium before game time.

YOUR ACTIONS
Affect Others

Whether you're a player on the field, or a fan in the stands, your actions affect others. If a player commits a penalty, his team suffers. If a fan leaves a bunch of trash in the stadium, someone has to pick it up. Think about the bigger picture.

HUMAN BEINGS
Are Creatures of Habit

I always walked the same route to the stadium, to get there the same amount of time before the game, to enjoy the quiet time before the game started.

Watch the people around you. You know a lot of what they do from your daily interactions.

MUSIC
Can Make You Happy

I always enjoy it when the band plays our fight song, not just because of school pride, but because it usually means we have just scored.

THE TELEVISION MUTE BUTTON

Is Not Just for When the Phone Rings

Let me be honest, I find most game announcers annoying. They talk about inane things during the game, when you really wish they'd just be quiet. God forbid some poor kid had a tragedy in his family because they'll never let him, or us, forget it. They mention it in every game the poor kid plays in. By the end of the first season of hearing it, you just want to say, "God bless the poor kid, but shut up about it already!" I think the media wants to make people cry.

I have rebelled. I will put the television on mute and turn the radio dial to my team's radio announcers, whom I enjoy. Not only do I get to watch the game, accompanied by announcers I like, I also get to know how the next play is going to turn out, because I hear it on the radio before I see it on television.

TALKING HEADS
Don't Know Everything

Some of the television guys are very pompous. They are the reason I rebelled with the mute button.

"Team" Goals Are More Important Than "I" Goals

The goal of a team in college football is of course, to win the national championship. My team currently has two that we won in 1993 and 1999. The two years we won it, we had quarterbacks who ultimately went on to win the award for college football's best player. However, these individuals gave all for their team, their main goals were for the team, and individual awards were an added benefit in their continual drive for excellence.

THE FANS
Love Animals

Football fans love animals. Look at how many teams have animal mascots. What mascots do fans usually vote as their favorites in sports magazines? The last time I heard, America's favorite was an animal.

HAVE
a Sense of Humor

Funny things happen during games. The mascots are funny, the fans are funny, and the media loves a coach who can give them a good quip now and then.

PRACTICE MAY NOT MAKE PERFECTION, but It Will Make You Better.

You didn't think the team just showed up to play on game day and magically knew all the plays, had their timing down, and were mechanically sound, did you? I thought not. Practice makes a player better.

You Are Not Always Going to Deal
With People You Like

Players are not always going to like other players, and coaches are not always going to like other coaches. There may be some antagonism between coaches and the media. It's a fact of life that you are not always going to like the people you have to deal with, but you can be the person who won't perpetuate the negativity.

Some People Are Never Going to Like You,
No Matter What You Do

Some people are never going to like you, regardless of how nice you are, how good a person you may be, or how high your goals are. Some people will find a small reason not to like you, even if it's just the fact that you play for another team and not theirs.

Most people want to be liked. Accepting that not everyone is going to like you is an important, but painful, lesson. It's particularly hard for kids. You have to set your goals, have your head on straight, and continue striving toward your better self. Accept that no one on this planet is liked by everyone.

RESPECT
Those that Have Gone Before You

One of the great things about college football is the respect for tradition. We fans like to honor those players, coaches, and others who have had an impact on our beloved team.

It saddens me as a fan when success comes and fans "hop on the bandwagon," but the moment the ride gets a little rough, they want to get rid of the coaches or players who in the overall scheme of things, put the program in the successful position it currently holds. Young fans are particularly prone to this. Some teams have built a tradition of excellence long enough that the younger fans have never had to sit through a seven and four or an eight and three season. I remember sitting through a few of those as the program was being built. I know that older fans have sat through worse. It's an example of how spoiled fans of successful teams get that I can even talk about a seven and four or eight and three season like it was hard times. Most teams would be ecstatic with such a record. Football success can be very cyclical. Have enough character as a fan to respect those who have gone before you. Respect those who built your program. Stick with that program. Stick with that program during tough times. Character lasts when the glitz is past.

GOD DOESN'T CARE
About Football

God doesn't care about football. If He did, He might have saved me "wide rights" over the years. God has more important things to do.

DON'T FORGET
the Ones Who Aren't in the Limelight

The mighty guys on the line don't get as much press as guys in other positions, but they are just as important. The game is won and lost in the trenches. Hats off to the tough ones on the offensive and defensive lines.

PEOPLE WILL OVERLOOK THINGS as Long as You Win

People will let you get away with a lot of stuff as long as you're winning. The second you stop winning, the things they overlooked will come back to haunt you. They will turn on you like a pack of dogs.

PEOPLE
Covet Success

Everyone wants to be successful, right? No kid goes to a school so he can say, "Our team lost every game we ever played in." There is nothing wrong with having goals and wanting to be successful in life. The important thing is how you go about obtaining that success. You can't let success become your idol. You can't let a "win at all costs" philosophy rule your life. Some things such as integrity and honor are more important than winning.

Some People
Have More Money Than Sense

It never ceases to amaze me what people will find to spend their money on. When you see some of the jewelry, clothes, cars, and houses successful people acquire, you just have to laugh. Why would a guy who is single need a house that darn big? I can see how some people wind up broke.

LOCATION
Matters

It is funny to me how I can buy a soda for a dollar at a store, but go to a stadium, and put that same drink in a cup, and it costs three.

Some People Use Sports as an Excuse
to Do Stupid Things

Think of all the stupid people who riot after ballgames. There are also people who get in fights after games, shoot people, run over people at burger joints, and a whole host of things.

DESPITE YOUR BEST EFFORTS, *Your Child Has His Own Mind*

Despite the fact that your child may go with you to all your team's games, he may still grow up to support another team. Kids do have a habit of growing up to do what they want.

Honor and Integrity
Last

Honor, integrity, and true friendship last. They'll be with you even if the money goes. Be a person of your word.

You Can Find a Statistic to Support Almost Anything You Want to Say

Depending on my purpose, I can find a statistic to support almost anything I want to say. If I want to praise my quarterback, I may want to use one statistic. If I want to say he's not playing well, I may quote another.

Think
Before You Speak

We live in an age of computers, satellites, televisions, and other technological advances unimaginable years ago. If a player or coach says something, it'll be on someone's web site almost before he's finished speaking. Consider your words carefully.

MONEY
Doesn't Make You Happy

If money equaled happiness, sports stars, rock stars, movie stars, and moguls should be the happiest people on the planet. Many of them earn more than regular working folks are ever going to see. Yet, a lot of them seem unhappy. Maybe they feel trapped.

Often, when people start making money, others start depending on them, so they feel they have to keep making it. They never stop running on the wheel. Maybe their trust has been abused, or they feel they can't trust new people because they fear they're only after their money. That brings us to the next lesson.

THERE ARE PEOPLE
Who Will Try to Get Close to People with Money

There are people who are only out for what they can get. There are false friends who only want to use you to get into clubs or get expensive gifts or cash. There are also people who will intentionally try to form a relationship with an athlete for the purposes of scoring a meal ticket.

I'm using athletes as an example, but this happens in regular life, as well. Some people are looking for someone to support them. It may sound harsh, but some people are lazy, useless drains on the resources of society.

AN EDUCATION
Is Important

College athletes are students. They need to have getting an education as their first priority, because as football fans, we've all seen players get hurt. What happens when you don't have football? An education will empower them when the days of gridiron glory are behind them.

DIVERSIFY
Your Holdings

A lot of athletes have other investments, such as restaurants, real estate, or other assets. Take this as a lesson for your life. Have other sources of income.

"Like" and "Respect"
Are Not the Same Thing

There are players and coaches fans respect for their talents, but don't like as people. There are players and coaches fans like as people, but they can't totally respect. The best situation is when you find people you can like and respect.

As Long as You Like Something, *You Can Talk About It a Lot*

I love football. I could talk about football all day. Even if I had to repeat myself because I'd run out of new material, I'd be happy just because I was talking about football.

SUCCESS
Can Affect a Lot of People

A player's success can affect his family, his friends, his community, and his world. Aside from the financial rewards of being successful, kids look up to a player. If he has a strong value system and a commitment to help make a better world, his influence can extend far beyond himself.

RETHINK,
If You're Not Happy

Sometimes a kid gets to the school that recruited him, realizes that he's homesick, or the situation on the team isn't what he thought it'd be. Sometimes he has to be strong enough to say, " I need to be in another situation right now." Rethink your situation if you're not happy.

Just Because the World's Going to Hell in a Handbasket, That Doesn't Mean I Have to Jump in and Sit on Their Lap

I'm still a young person, but even I can look back and see where values have changed over my lifetime. However, that does not mean that as a person, or as a fan, I have to lower my conduct or change my values to fit in with things that I don't agree with. I don't have to engage in fights or vandalism with other fans. I don't want to be liked so much that I feel I have to do things I'm not comfortable with, so others will like me. Stay true to your values, and surround yourself with people who will reinforce your high standards. Remember that you're always striving to be the best you can be.

The Boss Takes the Blame or Credit

Whether He Wants to or Not

In football, the head coach is the one who takes the blame when things are going badly, and gets the credit when they're not. The boss holds the ultimate responsibility, The coach can't watch over every assistant coach or every player all hours of the day and night. It's not physically possible. Let that kid make a bad decision that gets in the press, though, and they're all over the head coach. "He doesn't have control of his program," they'll say. In the end, all a coach can do is make sure his rules are known, try to exert a positive influence over the kid, and hope the kid has enough sense to see what's in his best interests.

SOME PEOPLE
Are Just out for Themselves.

Some players are just out to promote themselves. You can tell by what they say when the camera's put on them. There are a lot of "I" statements. It's all about them. An example is "They can't stop me." There was a four or five year span in the recent past where players liked to say, "I'm here to showcase my talents." Almost every game I watched, some kid was saying that. I was dying! I was so glad when they quit saying that, I could hardly stand it. Football is a team sport, and for team success, say goodbye to the "I."

SOMETIMES
You Have to Cut Ties with People

Some people will not help themselves. They will not let you help them. Athletes, unfortunately, live out much of their personal drama under the glaring eye of the media. Some are on a path to personal destruction, and until they decide, in their own minds, that they need to make changes, they cannot be helped. Some act out during games, and become such a detriment to themselves and their teams, that ties have to be severed. It's a sad situation, particularly when a kid so obviously has talent and potential. One person cannot be allowed to drag down a whole team.

BE
a Person of Your Word

In football, a coach can live or die by this one. If he promises a kid a scholarship, and the kid comes to his school, he needs to make sure he keeps his word. The program's integrity is adversely affected if kids can't believe what a coach tells them. Word will get around, and kids won't want to come to that school. Coaches may even have problems with each other if honesty becomes an issue.

TRASH TALK
Is Meaningless

Trash talk means nothing. It is just one more thing players do to try to get in opposing players' heads. Usually, the more mature players don't need to do all that talking. They know that knocking the crap out of them during the play pretty much says it all.

I hate to admit it, but trash talk does work on some people, in football and in life. Less mature players fall for it. Players who are weak of mind fall for it. People in your office fall for it. Keep positive thoughts in your mind and remember trash talk is just that, "talk."

SOMETIMES IT'S BETTER
to Say
as Little as Possible

When emotions are running high, it's a big rivalry game, or the team's going through adverse circumstances, sometimes it's better to say as little as possible. Don't give other teams bulletin board fodder. Just say, "I hope to play well."

When You're Looking for the Keys to Success, Go Deep.
Look for Discipline, Enthusiasm, Education, and Persistence

Players who are disciplined can't help but be successful. They realize that sacrifices must be made to succeed, and they make those sacrifices willingly.

Enthusiasm keeps the power on the "up" position. Players who are enthusiastic make other players enthusiastic, too. Players who know the joy of football and love being out there, will play harder. Upsets are made with enthusiasm.

Education is important to a kid both on the field and off.

Persistence is sometimes the only thing that separates a successful team from an unsuccessful one. A persistent team keeps coming all sixty minutes. There's no "quit" in them. Your team ain't legit, unless they've got no "quit."

You Can't Judge Right or Wrong

with a Clock or a Calendar

Some people have situational ethics. They manage to get by with that, a lot of times, but they lose respect. You can't judge right or wrong with a clock or a calendar. You can't say, "It was wrong for me to do that ten minutes ago, but now it's okay." It's always wrong to cheat to get players, to lie to players or coaches, to intentionally inflict injury on a player to put him out of the game, or any of a host of other things. Draw your line and keep it drawn.

SOMETIMES
You Need a Good "Y" Chromosome

It's unfortunate, but a lot of good games are on at the same time. Therefore, I have to resort to deciding which game is my main game and which one I flip to during commercials. My remote will only allow me to set this up to flip between two channels. One night my father told me he was planning to flip between not two, but three games! Suitably impressed by his ambition, though somewhat dubious of his chances of success, I joked with him that I could never hope to gain his level of expertise with the remote control, because I was missing that important Y chromosome!

Just as men learn not to interrupt women when they're on that quest for the perfect purse, women learn to never come between a man and his remote control! I can only dream of reaching my father's level of expertise.

PUNCTUALITY
Is Key

It's important for a player to get to practice, meetings, and games on time. It's important for fans to get to games on time. Punctuality is important.

To me, punctuality shows respect for another person and his time. It says that you know that others have things they could be doing besides waiting on you. Emergencies are unavoidable, but most of the time, late people don't plan.

PRAISE IN PUBLIC,
Criticize in Private

Coaches lose respect if they criticize coaches or players in public. If they have something nice to say, they should let everyone know, but keep the negative things for later.

You may have seen this in your own workplace. Watch how bosses criticize or praise their employees.

THE INMATES
Can't Run the Asylum

The coach, or the boss, dictates the rules and procedures by which a team or unit is governed. While suggestions for improvements may be welcome, players or workers cannot start doing their own thing, trying to run the organization. If you don't like the way an organization is run, you do have three options. You can accept the rules and learn to live with the current system. You can attempt to effect positive changes in the system. You can leave.

PEOPLE CAN'T BE HELPED

Unless They Want to Be Helped.

Unless a player admits he needs and wants help, he can't be helped. Efforts to talk fall on deaf ears. Helping hands are left ungrasped.

ALWAYS
Have a Little Money on You

It's always nice to have a little money on you. You never know what surprises life will bring. Have the pay phone and cab money available. You might have a flat, or want to buy a snack.

ALWAYS
Have Some Scrap Paper on You

You never know whom you'll bump into on game day. Have some scrap paper to write down the phone number for that old friend from high school.

HAVE *Fun*

Have fun at the game, at the restaurant, or at home. Wherever you watch your favorite team play, have a good time.

CONSIDER
the Source

When you hear stories on the television or radio, talk to people, or read articles in the newspaper or on the computer, consider the source. Ask yourself, "Is this person objective? What is his purpose in saying this? Do I already know this person does not like this athlete, coach, or team?"

HAVE
Varied Interests and Goals

There is life after football, for players and fans. Have other interests and goals that are not related to football. It makes us more interesting people.

BE A GIVER,
and Not a Taker

Give as you've been blessed. Don't take from everybody. Give without expectation of anything in return. Many athletes give back to their communities. Return the blessings.

Some Days You'll Lose, No Matter How Hard You Play

Some games, things just don't go your way. One of the best lessons a player or person can learn is how to deal with a loss with class. It's painful to know that you lost a game despite your best efforts, but you just can't win all your games, all the time.

SOME PEOPLE
Need More Outside Motivation Than Others.

Some players need little or no outside motivation. They fire up their own furnace. Others have all the talent in the world, but are severely lacking in motivation. Parents, players, and coaches can help with that.

Loyalty
Is Important

One of the best things I ever saw was a television interview with one of our former quarterbacks talking about he still got chills when he walked through the tunnel at Doak Campbell Stadium. That was one of the most wonderful things I ever heard. I love him for that.

IT IS HARD
to Watch
Dreams Get Crushed

The hardest part of watching a football game is sitting there when a young guy gets injured. You know they're counting on playing professional ball, and some injuries can keep those dreams from being realized.

If You Have The Desire in Your Heart, Put the Knowledge in Your Head to Lay Those Train Tracks to Your Dreams.

Every little bit of effort you exert, every bit of knowledge you collect, helps you move one step closer to the attainment of your goals. I call these efforts "laying those train tracks to your dreams."

ADVERSITY
Can Bring Out the Best in People

When the team's down, that's when you see what your team's got. If a team's got character, adversity is going to bring forth their best efforts.

ADVERSITY
Can Bring Out the Worst in People.

When a team's down, if they don't have any character, or any pride, you can see it. You'll watch a game, and you can almost pinpoint down to an exact moment when you see them quit. Adversity's knocks either make you get up or give up.

You Never Know What They Can Do
Until You Give Them a Chance

Some players sit on the bench for years, then one day, they get their chance to get in the game, and it's wonderful! It's magic time! You never know what a kid can do until you give him a chance.

SIMPLE GAME DAY EATS
Are the Best

Some people prepare elaborate dishes for tailgating or home viewing. I don't like to cook. If I ever get married, my husband and I won't have to live on love, as long as we've got a microwave. If you ever hear me talk about getting out a double boiler, though, start looking for the Four Horsemen of the Apocalypse, because the end is nigh. That being said, I stick with game day snack standards such as chips and dip, wings, or pizza.

DOPE
Makes Duds

Drugs ruin lives. The media's full of stories of money blown, families broken, and lives in shambles. Dope makes duds.

ACT WITH LOVE, and *Good Things Will Happen*

I spend the majority of my working hours at my office. Since I'm there so much, I like to decorate it with items I find that delight or inspire me in some way. These items include various Florida State posters and such. I have one wall, my "Florida State wall," on which I hang nothing but my Florida State stuff.

A nice insurance man out of the Tallahassee office once visited us and he and I started discussing football. Something of my enthusiasm must have communicated itself to him, because he said he knew someone on the coaching staff, and he'd get me an autographed picture of Bobby Bowden. Now, dear reader, if my love of Bobby Bowden has somehow failed to be communicated up to this point, let me state it plainly here. I love Coach Bowden.

A couple of weeks later, I received an envelope from the Florida State Athletic Department which contained an autographed picture of Coach Bowden.

This insurance man's unexpected kindness meant a lot to me because my one regret was, and still is, that I never got to meet Coach Bowden while I was attending Florida State. Of course, if I actually met him, I'd either be bereft of words or I'd get too excited and sound like an idiot. My voice gets high when I get excited, so I'd probably sound like a dolphin on helium.

My point is that I acted out of love, and this insurance man responded with a spontaneous kindness.

Don't Compare Yourself with Others

Comparing yourself with another person just leads to disappointment. Players may have similarities, but comparing one to another is just as pointless.

I figured out a long time ago that I was never going to be taller, or have bigger goodies. That's all right. I'll just be me. I am still trying to find the perfect purse to go with the "best me" I'm trying to bring into being, though.

People Build You Up, Then Tear You Down

It's sad but true; people seem to love to build players, actors, or others up into these great big things, only to take great glee in tearing them down.

PROFILE OF THE AUTHOR
as a Football Fan

NAME: **Charlotte Barnes**

SCIENTIFIC NAME: **Footballus Fanaticus**

NATURAL HABITAT: **Doak Campbell Stadium in Tallahassee, Florida; or on the chair in the living room somewhere in Florida**

TEAMS FAVORED: **Florida State University, University of Alabama**

SYMPTOMS OF FOOTBALLUS FANATICUS: **Turned down a date to watch football**

Resents friends who schedule events on game day

Would rather meet football coaches than governors or presidents

Turned hurricane evacuation into a pilgrimage to the Bear Bryant Museum, Bryant-Denny Stadium, and Legion Field

Sat in stadium two hours before game time

Seen so many Bobby Bowden interviews that "dadgummit" has become a permanent part of her personal lexicon

Quotes sports magazines so much that acquaintances think that "Athlon" and "Lindy" must be some relatives of hers who know a lot about football

PERSONAL GOALS RELATING TO FOOTBALL:
- *Go to a Florida State Media Day*

- *See a game in every stadium in the Southeastern Conference*

- *Go to a University of Alabama football game*

PERSONAL GOALS NOT RELATED TO FOOTBALL:
- *Would like to promote treating others with respect and kindness*

- *Would like to help promote her alma mater, Florida State University, in whatever capacity possible*

- *Would like to help promote all aspects of the arts, both in Florida, and nationally*